Mel Bay Presents

Classic Guitar
for the Young Beginner

By William Bay

MW00368581

CD CONTENTS

1	Tuning	25	Finger Builder	49	Chord Songs	73	Classic Dance
2	Play E	26	Flower Song	50	Re-Count	74	Low Gear
3	Rest Study	27	Lyric Waltz	51	Melancholy Dance	75	We Wish You a Merry Christmas
4	E in 3/4 time	28	Dotted half Song	52	Puppet Waltz	76	Arpeggio Study
5	I Love Eating Donuts!	29	All Smiles	53	Railroad Bill	77	Angelina Baker
6	Don't Step on Alligators!	30	Running the Strings	54	Rise and Shine	78	The Water is Wide
7	Eating Pizza Makes Me Happy	31	Count Again	55	Lonesome Valley	79	Spanish Song
8	8th Note Study #2	32	Wide Spaces	56	Our Team Will Shine Tonight	80	Can Can
9	3/4 Study	33	Climbing the Strings	57	The Roving Gambler	81	Polovetsian Dance
10	Cimbing Stairs	34	Staircase	58	This Little Light of Mine	82	Hey, Ho, Nobody's Home
11	I Love Eating Pizza	35	Three String Study	59	Precious Memories	83	Eighth Rest
12	One And-A-Two And-A	36	Friends	60	Early American Hymn	84	Matty Groves
13	Out West	37	Classic Theme	61	Come and Go with Me	85	Forest Green
14	Waltz	38	Study #2	62	Salty Dog Blues	86	Once in Royal David's City
15	The Count	39	Study #4	63	Steal Away	87	Minuet by Bach
16	Mix Up	40	Spanish Dance	64	I Know Where I'm Going	88	Waltzing Matilda
17	B-E	41	Right Hand Study	65	Down Shift	89	Ding, Dong, Merrily on High
18	3/4 C-B	42	Rock Feeling	66	What's up?	90	Auld Lang Syne
19	Climbing	43	Indian Prayer	67	Shifting Gears	91	Finlandia Theme
20	C-B-C	44	Good King Wenceslas	68	Song	92	Waltz by Chopin
21	Surprise Song	45	African Hymn	69	Hometown Waltz	93	German Hymn
22	Sailing	46	Bucking Bronco	70	Guitar Polka		
23	Walking Over Hills	47	Count	71	Volga Boatmen		
24	Waltz	48	Minor Melody	72	Little Dance		

1 2 3 4 5 6 7 8 9 0

Visit us on the Web at www.melbay.com — E-mail us at email@melbay.com

How to Select a Guitar

When selecting a guitar for a child, it is essential that the instrument obtained is not too big for the student. For most children, I recommend a student-size or a 3/4 size classic guitar. In addition, you must make certain that the neck is not too wide. Be sure to take the student in and let the student hold the instrument to see if it is manageable. Also, check the strings to make certain that they are not too high off the fingerboard at the nut, or first fret (consult the parts of the guitar diagram to see where this is). Also, your teacher may help you check whether or not there are string buzzes or some other problem with the instrument. Most of the student-model guitars being made today are of a very good quality, and many of the problems which used to plague beginning guitarists are no longer concerns.

The Guitar and its Parts

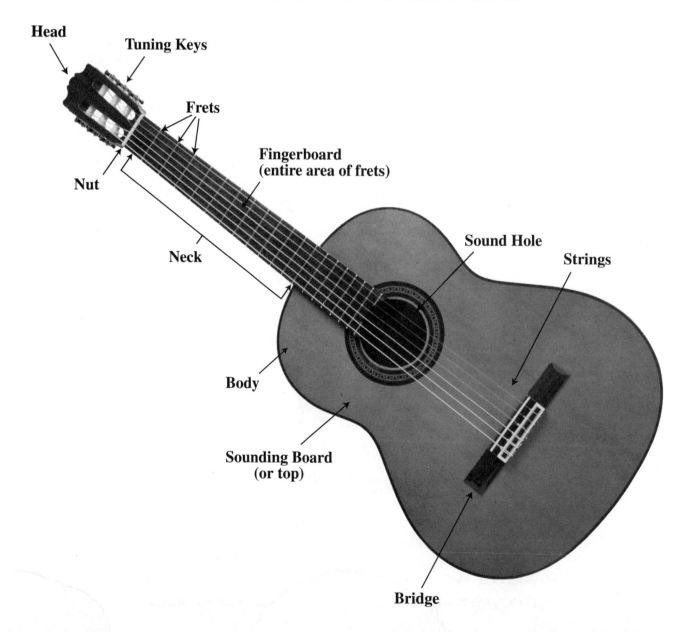

How to Hold the Guitar

Classic guitarists rest the intrumcnt on their left leg. While this position may be more uncomfortable in the beginning, it does have certain advantages. In this position, the left elbow hangs naturally and thereby gives the left hand flexibility. Also, the right hand fits comfortably on the strings. In the classic playing position, a footstool* may he needed in order to raise the left leg. Generally speaking, the classic playing position facilitates left-hand fingering because it brings the neck of the guitar closer to the body.

*The types of footstools pictured here may be purchased at your local music store.

A-Frame Adjustable Support

The use of the "A-Frame" adjustable support allows you great flexibility in adjusting the guitar. We recommend it because it allows you to find the most comfortable and beneficial position.

**The adjustable support shown here is the A-Frame, which is available through Mel Bay Publications 1-800-8 MEL BAY.

Right Hand Position

The right arm should pivot approximately at the widest point on the instrument. Make certain that the elbow and wrist are loose. The right arm should feel comfortable to you. The tone will vary depending upon where the strings are plucked. The closer that we play to the fingerboard, the more mellow the tone. The sound is correspondingly sharper as we play closer to the bridge. The fingers should be held loosely so that flexibility can be attained. Make certain that your wrist and fingers are not held in a rigid, stiff manner.

Right Hand Fingers Touching String

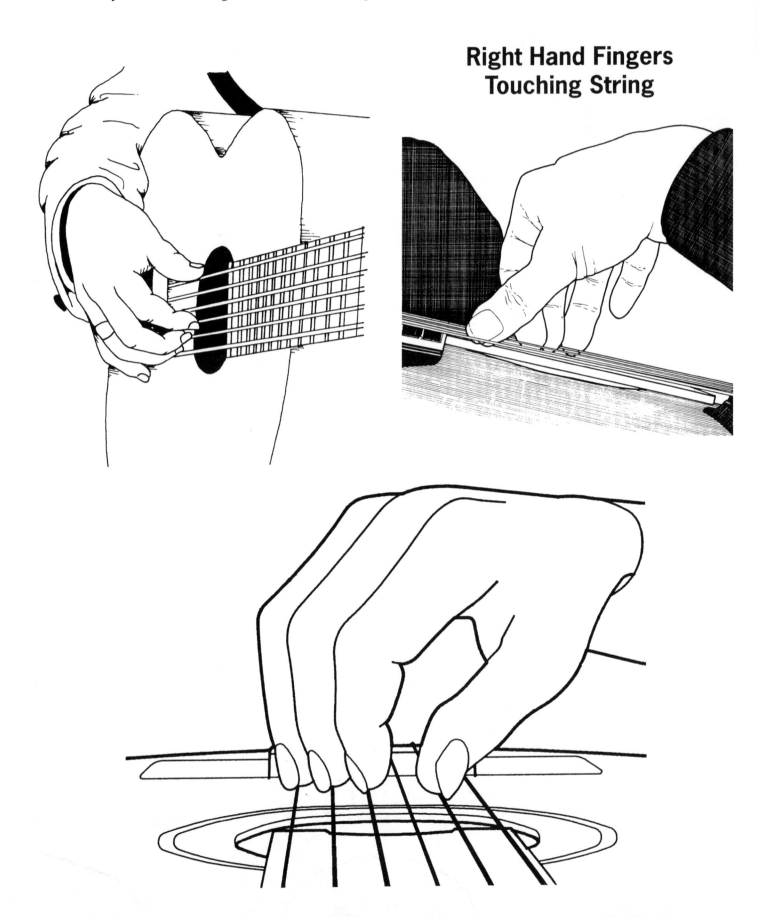

Left Hand Positioning

To begin with, keep the left elbow and wrist relaxed. Avoid positioning that strains and tightens your left wrist and elbow. The important thing to remember is to place the left hand so that the hand is arched and so that the fingers can fall straight down on the strings. Greater technique can he obtained by pressing down on the strings with the tips of the fingers than with the fleshy part. Also. it is important to bring the fingers directly down on the strings so that part of the finger does not accidentally touch and muffle one of the other strings.

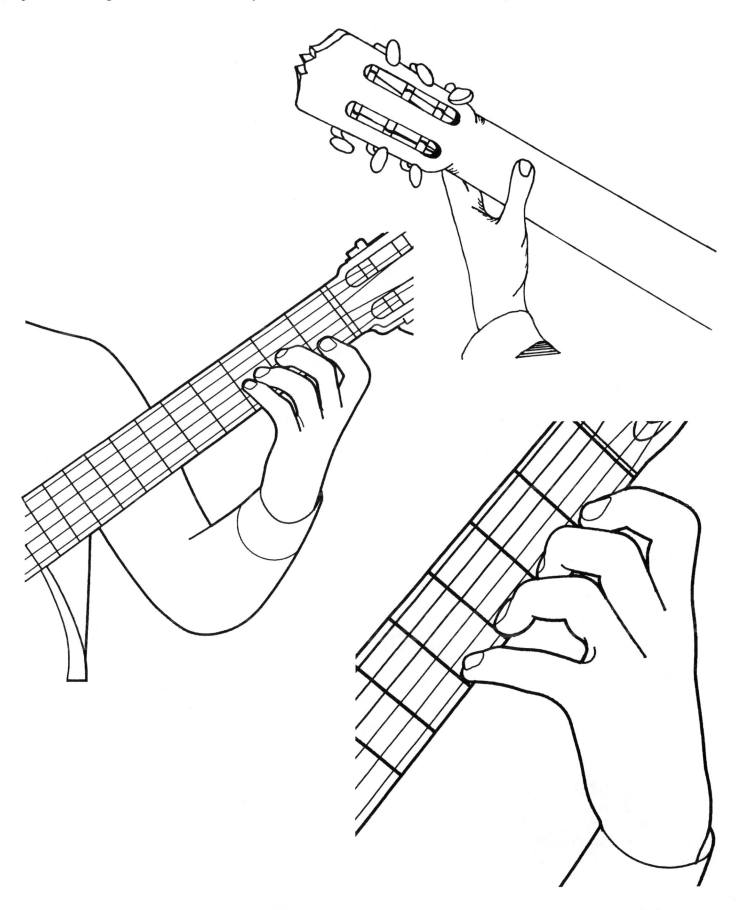

Tuning the Guitar

6th /↗ ↑ ↖\ 1st
5th | \ 2nd
4th 3rd

 Tr.1   **Listen to track #1 of your CD and tune up as follows!**

1st String – E

2nd String – B

3rd String – G

4th String – D

5th String – A

6th Strin – Low E

Electronic Guitar Tuner

Electronic Guitar Tuners are available at your music store. They are a handy device and highly recommended.

Left Hand Fingering   Right Hand Fingering

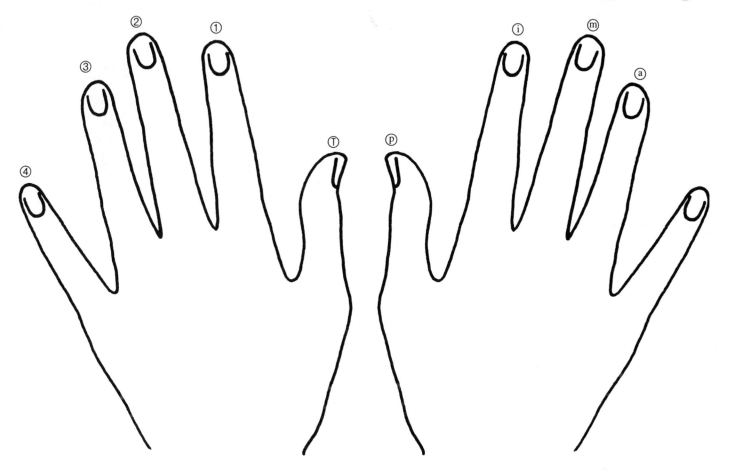

Right-hand finger symbols are derived from Spanish. The letters stand for:

Symbol	Spanish	English
p	Pulgar	Thumb
i	Índice	Index Finger
m	Medio	Middle Finger
a	Anular	Ring Finger

Our First Note

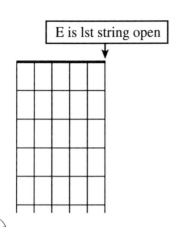

E is 1st string open

E

Open

The 1st string on the guitar is called the high **E String**. Our first note is E-open 1st string.

Play E with Middle Finger (m)

Tr.2

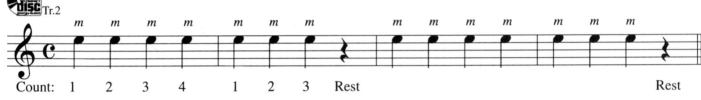

Count: 1 2 3 4 1 2 3 Rest Rest

Play E with Index Finger (i)

This type of note is called a **quarter note**. It gets 1 count.

Rest Rest

Alternate Middle and Index Fingers

Repeat the above example 3 times. Rest Rest

Rest Study

Tr.3

Count: 1 2 Rest Rest 1 2

E in ¾ Time

Tr.4

Count: 1 2 3 1 2 Rest

Counting Song

Count: 1   2   (3)   4   1   2   (3)   4

> On the following song we will play a new type of note called an eighth note. It looks like this ♪ or this ♫ or this ♫♫. Eighth notes get only 1/2 the time a quarter note ♩ gets. Say the following song and play it.

I Love Eating Donuts!

Tr.5

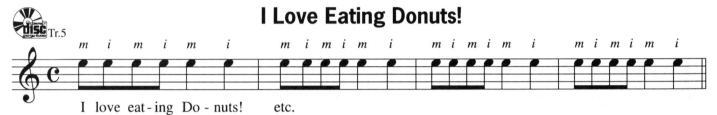

I love eat-ing Do-nuts!   etc.

Note: each exercise should be played several times to insure correct rhythm and clean right-hand fingering. Listen to the companion recording to hear these studies!

Don't Step on Alligators!
(Say and Play)

Tr.6

Don't step on al-li-ga-tors!   etc.

Eating Pizza Makes Me Happy
(Say and Play)

Tr.7

Eat-ing Piz-za makes me hap-py.   etc.

A New Note

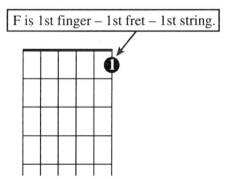

F is 1st finger – 1st fret – 1st string.

F

F is 1st finger, first fret, on 1st string.

E-F

E-F $\frac{3}{4}$

E-F-F-E

Study #4

E-F-E-F

F-E-F-E

8th Note Study #1

8th Note Study #2

* **C** = 4 beats per measure
  $\frac{3}{4}$ = 3 beats per measure

New Note

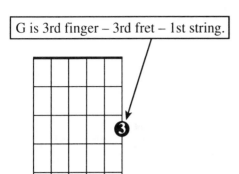

G is 3rd finger – 3rd fret – 1st string.

G

G is 3rd finger, 3rd fret, 1st string.

Play G

E-G

F-G

¾ Study

Tr.9

Climbing Stairs

Tr.10

1st String Studies

Chasing Notes

Up We Go

I Love Eating Pizza

See Saw

Marching

Don't Step on Alligators

Mimi Song

One And-A-Two And-A

Note Values

When a note appears we play		When a rest appears, we do **not** play!	

Quarter note

Gets 1 beat

Draw Quarter notes

A quarter note gets_____beats?

Quarter rest

Gets 1 beat

Draw Quarter rests

A quarter rest gets_____beat?

Whole note

Gets 4 counts

Draw whole notes

A whole note gets_____beats?

Whole note rest

Gets 4 beats

Draw whole note rests

A whole rest gets_____beats?

notice that it hangs down from line 2

Half note

Gets 2 counts

Draw half notes

A half note gets_____beats?

Half note rest

Gets 2 counts

Draw half note rests

A half note rest gets_____beats?

notice that it sits upon line 3

Eighth Note

Gets 1/2 beat

Draw eighth notes

An eighth note gets_____beat?

Eighth rest

Gets 1/2 beat

Draw eighth rests

An eighth note gets_____beat?

Quiz

What kind of note? Quarter ____ ____ ____ ____ ____ ____ ____ ____ ____ ____ ____

How many beats?   1   ____ ____ ____ ____ ____ ____ ____ ____ ____ ____ ____

Counting Songs

Out West

Waltz

The Count

Mix Up

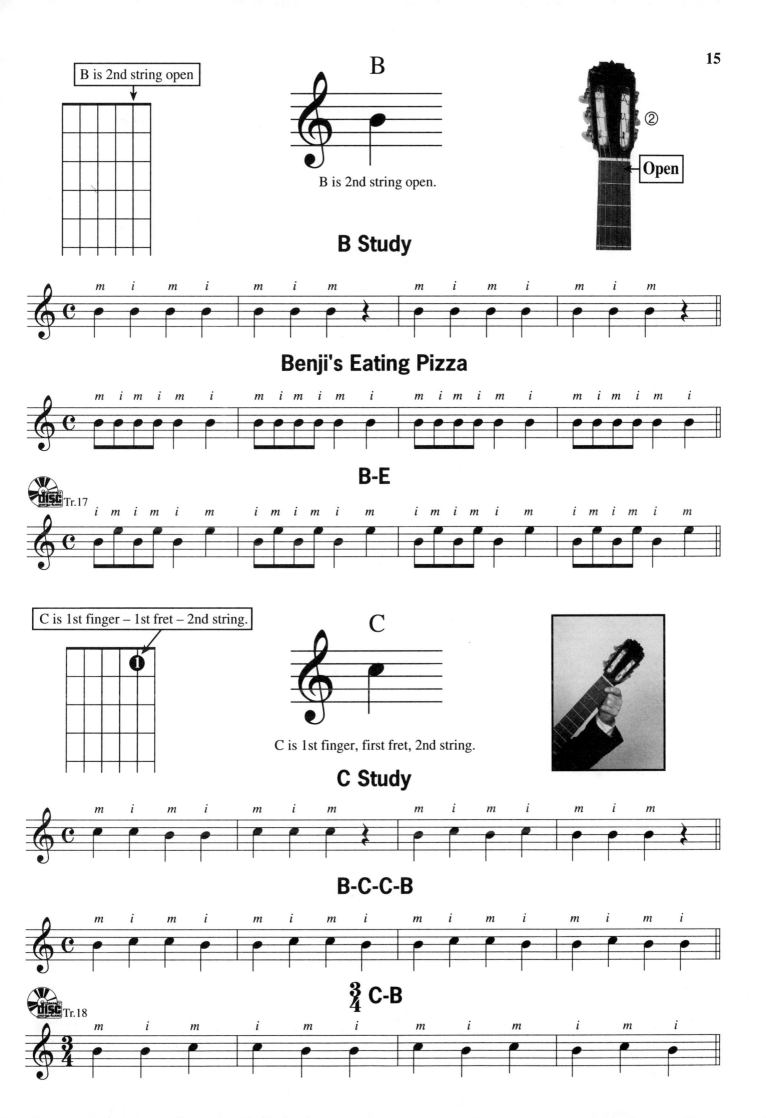

B is 2nd string open

B

B is 2nd string open.

Open

B Study

Benji's Eating Pizza

B-E

Tr.17

C is 1st finger – 1st fret – 2nd string.

C

C is 1st finger, first fret, 2nd string.

C Study

B-C-C-B

¾ C-B

Tr.18

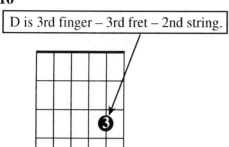

D is 3rd finger – 3rd fret – 2nd string.

D is 3rd finger, third fret, 2nd string.

Play D

D-B-C

D-C-B

Climbing

 Tr.19

C-B-C

Tr.20

Surprise Song

Sailing

Walking Over Hills

Waltz

Finger Builder

Dotted Half Note

A dotted half note receives 3 beats.

Flower Song

Lyric Waltz

Dotted Half Song

Two String Study

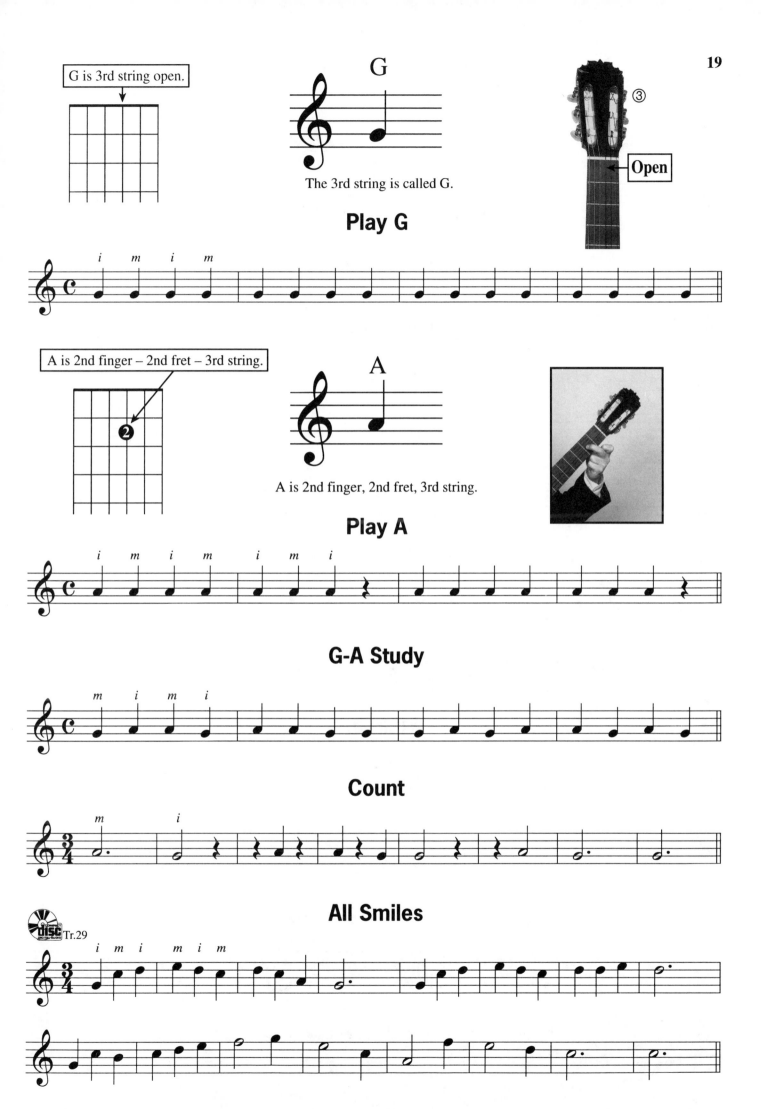

G is 3rd string open.

G

The 3rd string is called G.

Open

Play G

A is 2nd finger – 2nd fret – 3rd string.

A

A is 2nd finger, 2nd fret, 3rd string.

Play A

G-A Study

Count

All Smiles

Tr.29

Running the Strings

Count Again

Wide Spaces

Climbing the Strings

Staircase

Three String Study

Friends

Tr.36

Classic Theme

[Note the use of the Third Finger of the Right Hand (a)]

Tr.37

3rd Finger Study #1

Study #2

Study #3

Study #4

Study #5

Study #6

Mix Up

Also play this study using *a m i*

Arpeggio Studies

Arpeggio Study #1

Hold left hand 1st finger down and let tones ring.

Study #2

Study #3

Study #4

Spanish Dance

Arpeggio Study #5

Arpeggio Study #6

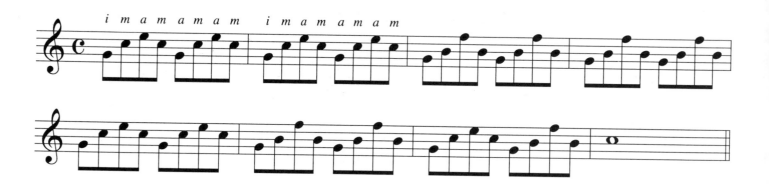

Right Hand Study

Mixed Study

Speed Study

Rock Feeling

Tr.42

Indian Prayer

Tr.43

Good King Wenceslas

Tr.44

African Hymn

Tr.45

The Fourth String

D is the 4th string open.

D

D is the 4th string open.

④ Open

Play D

i   m   i   m

E is 2nd finger – 2nd fret – 4th string.

②

E

A is 2nd finger, 2nd fret, 4th string.

Play E

i   m   i   m

D-E

m   i   m   i

F is 3rd finger – 3rd fret – 4th string.

③

F

F is 3rd finger, 3rd fret, 4th string.

Play F

i   m   i   m   i   m   i

Use of the Thumb (P)

Play each note in the following study with the thumb.

D-E-F

p   p   p   p   p   p

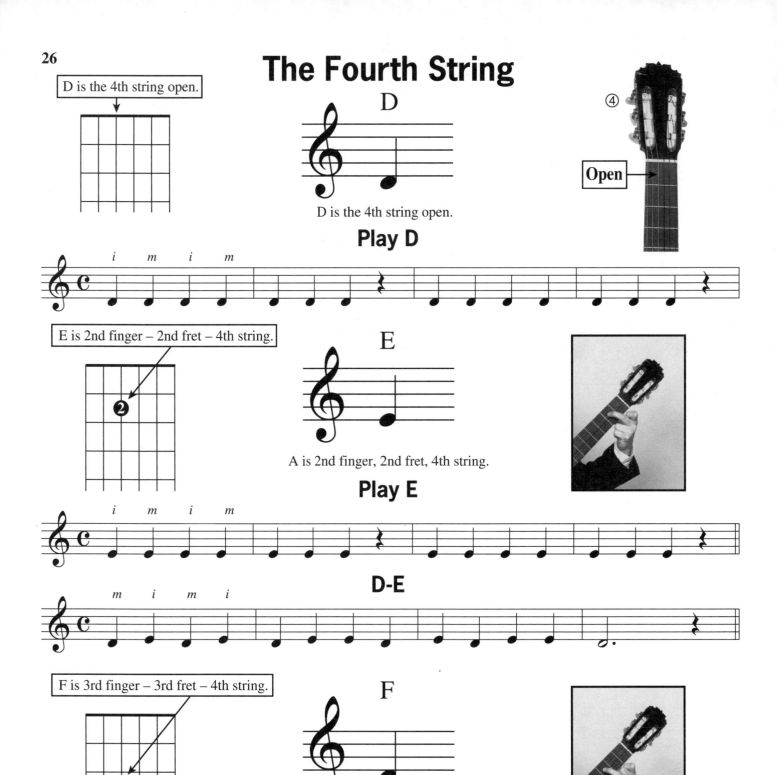

Eighth Note Study

Mystery

Thumb Study

Pulgar Waltz

Thumb Builder

Bucking Bronco

Tr.46

Count

Minor Melody

Chord Song

Re-Count

Melancholy Dance

Puppet Waltz

The Tie

A tie is a curved line that joins two or more notes of the same pitch. When you see a tie, only pick the first note.

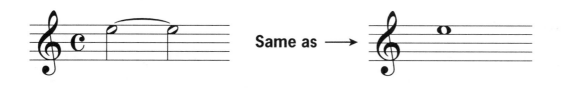

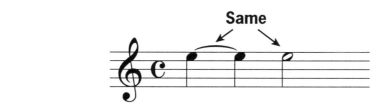

Railroad Bill

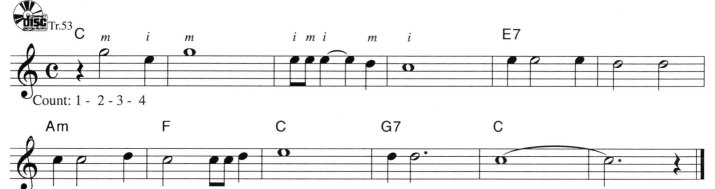

Rise and Shine

Pick-Up Notes

Some songs start with less than a full 4 beat measure. These starting notes are called a "Pick-up."

Taps

Count: 4 & 1 - 2 - 3 - 4 &

Reville

Count: 4 1 - 2 & 3 - 4

Lonesome Valley

Tr.55

Accompaniment
Chords:

Count: 3 4 1 - 2 - 3 - 4 1 - 2 - 3 - 4

Dotted Quarter Notes

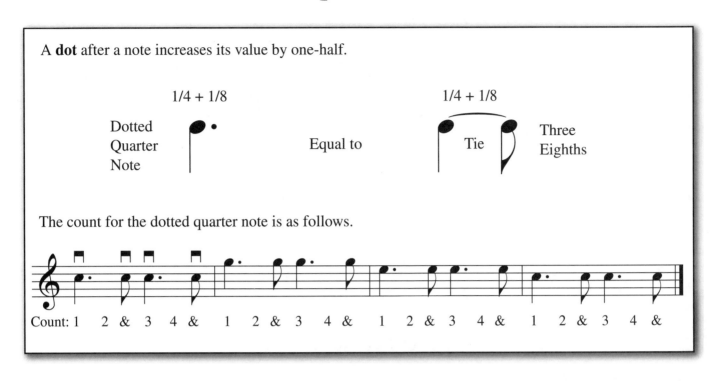

A **dot** after a note increases its value by one-half.

The count for the dotted quarter note is as follows.

Our Team Will Shine Tonight

The Roving Gambler

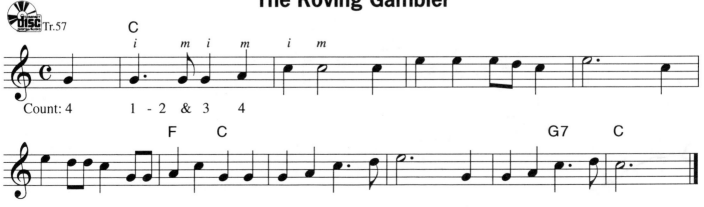

More Solos

Come and Go with Me

Salty Dog Blues

Steal Away

I Know Where I'm Going

Notes on the 5th String

A is the 5th string open.

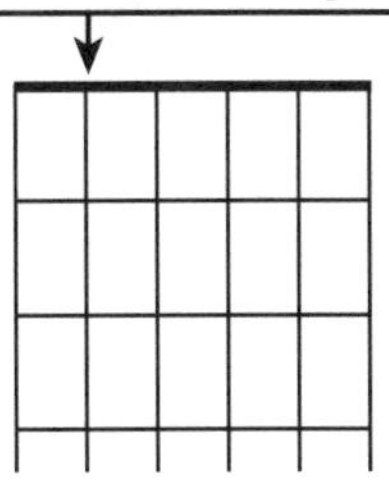

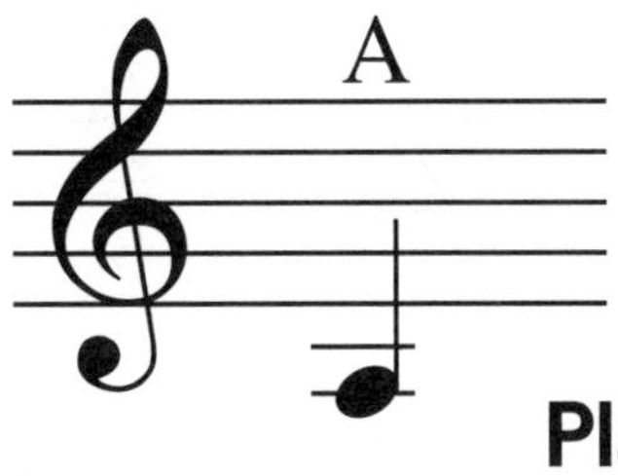

A is the 5th string open.

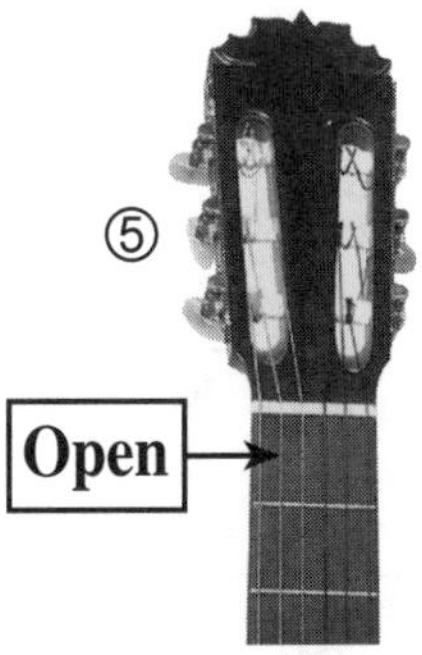

⑤

Open

Play A

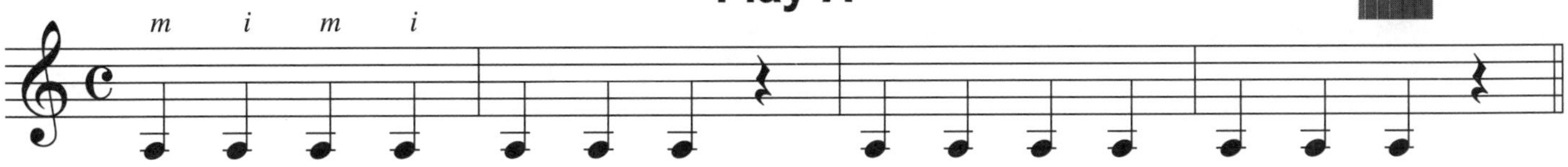

m i m i

B is 2nd finger – 2nd fret – 5th string.

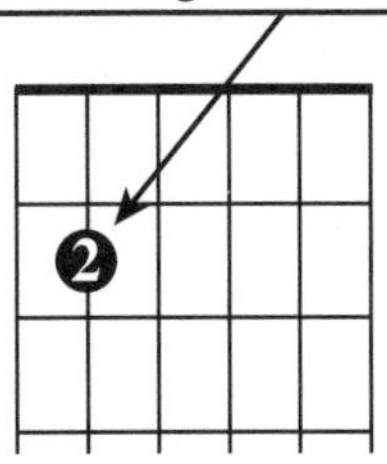

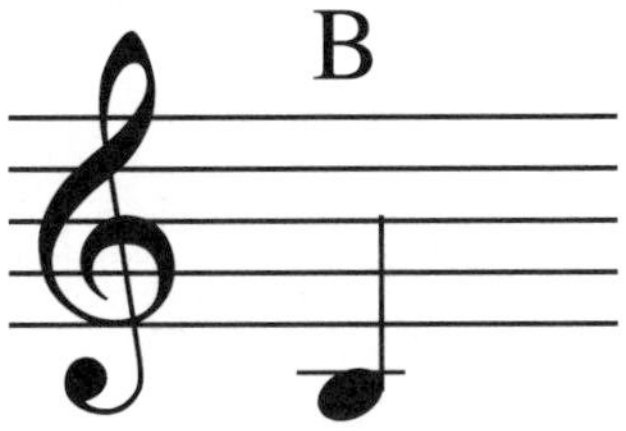

❷

B is 2nd finger, 2nd fret, 5th string.

Play B

A-B

C is 3rd finger – 3rd fret – 5th string.

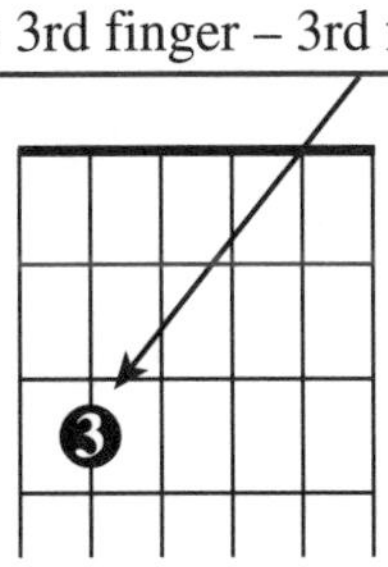

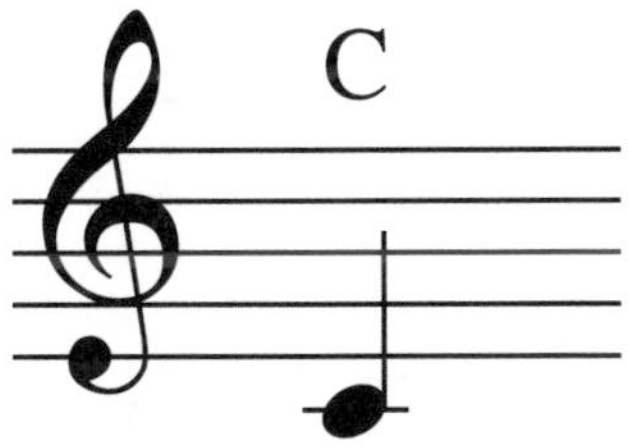

❸

C is 3rd finger, 3rd fret, 5th string.

Play C

i m i m

5th String Song

p

A String Study #1

p

Low A

Hometown Waltz

Guitar Polka

C Scale Study

Volga Boatmen

Arpeggio Studies

Hold left hand fingers down while arpeggio is being played.

Little Dance

Arpeggio Song

Right Hand Study

Play with both fingerings

W. Bay

Classic Dance

Tr.73

Low Gear

Tr.74

Notes on the 6th String

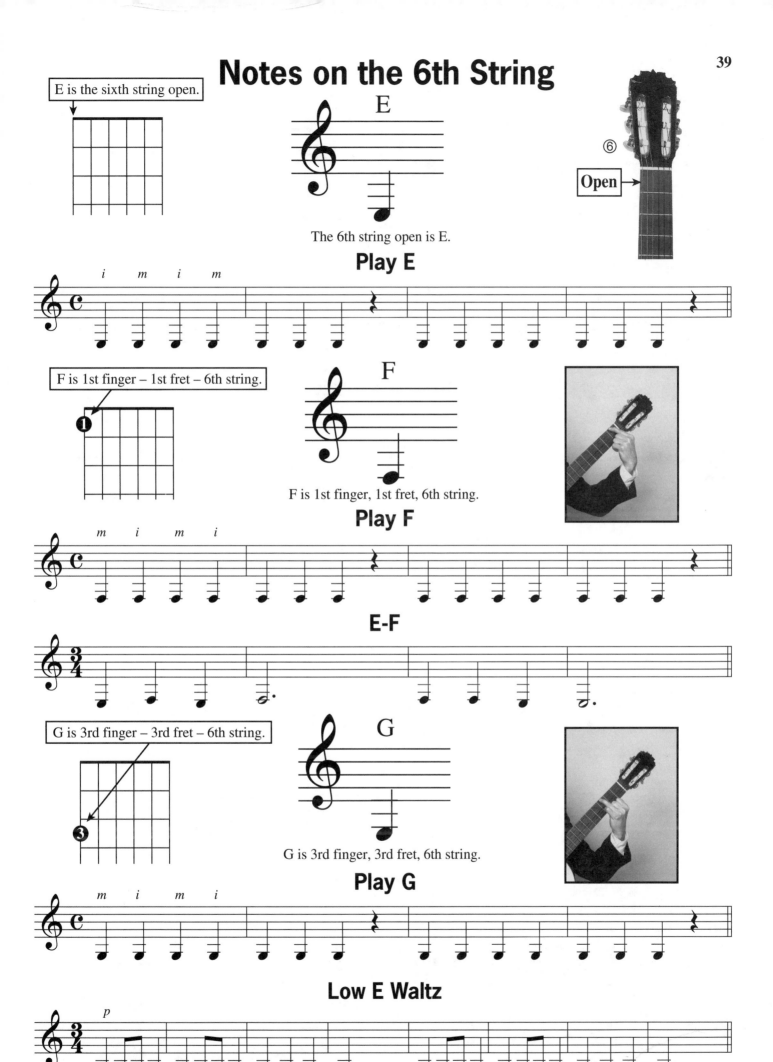

E is the sixth string open.

The 6th string open is E.

Play E

F is 1st finger – 1st fret – 6th string.

F is 1st finger, 1st fret, 6th string.

Play F

E-F

G is 3rd finger – 3rd fret – 6th string.

G is 3rd finger, 3rd fret, 6th string.

Play G

Low E Waltz

We Wish You A Merry Christmas

Arpeggio Study

C Scale Study #1

C Scale Study 2

Note Review

Angelina the Baker

The Water Is Wide

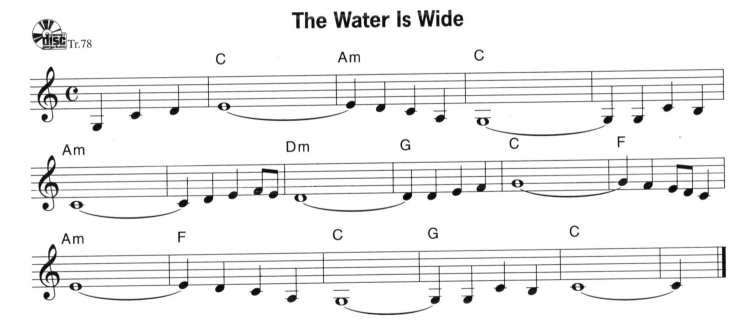

Spanish Song

3 New Notes-F Sharp

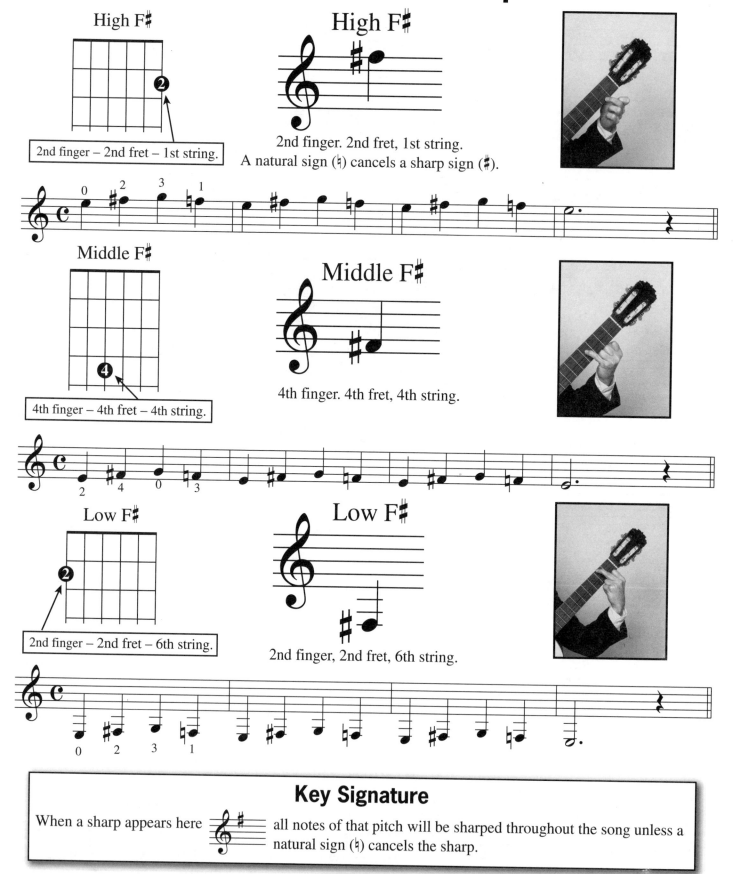

High F#

2nd finger – 2nd fret – 1st string.

High F#

2nd finger. 2nd fret, 1st string.
A natural sign (♮) cancels a sharp sign (♯).

Middle F#

4th finger – 4th fret – 4th string.

Middle F#

4th finger. 4th fret, 4th string.

Low F#

2nd finger – 2nd fret – 6th string.

Low F#

2nd finger, 2nd fret, 6th string.

Key Signature

When a sharp appears here all notes of that pitch will be sharped throughout the song unless a natural sign (♮) cancels the sharp.

G Scale

Can Can

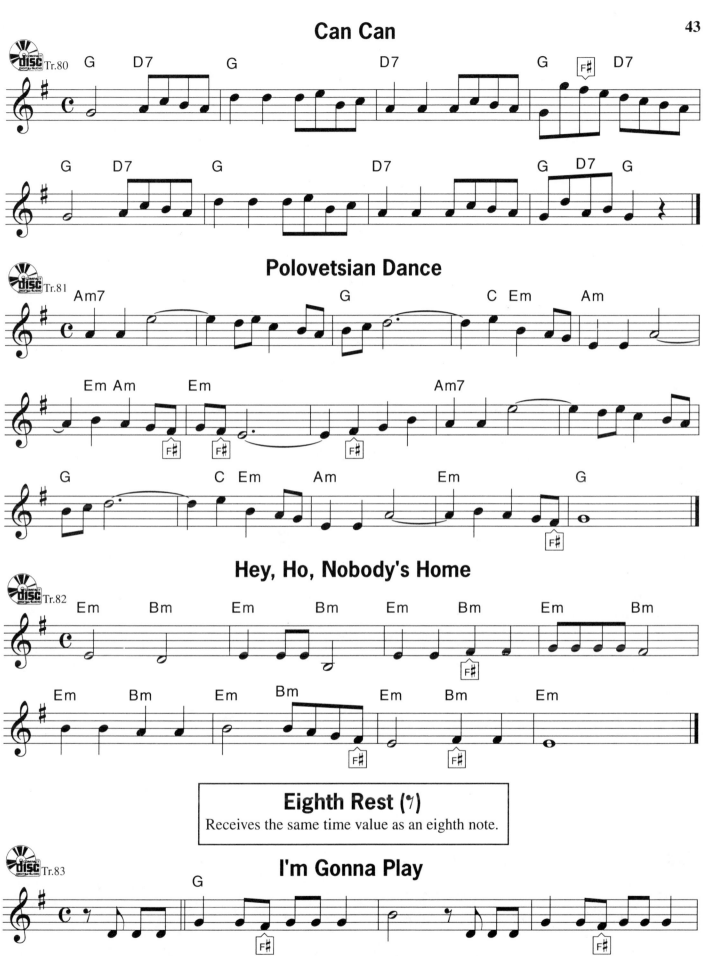

Polovetsian Dance

Hey, Ho, Nobody's Home

Eighth Rest (𝄾)
Receives the same time value as an eighth note.

I'm Gonna Play

Remember - if F♯ is in the key signature, all F's will be sharped unless a natural sign (♮) is in front of the F.

Matty Groves

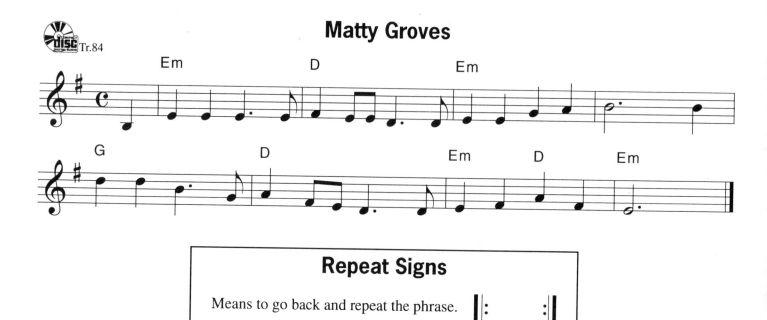

Repeat Signs

Means to go back and repeat the phrase. ‖: :‖

Forest Green

Once in Royal David's City

Minuet by Bach

Tr.87

Waltzing Matilda

Tr.88

Ding, Dong, Merrily on High

Tr.89

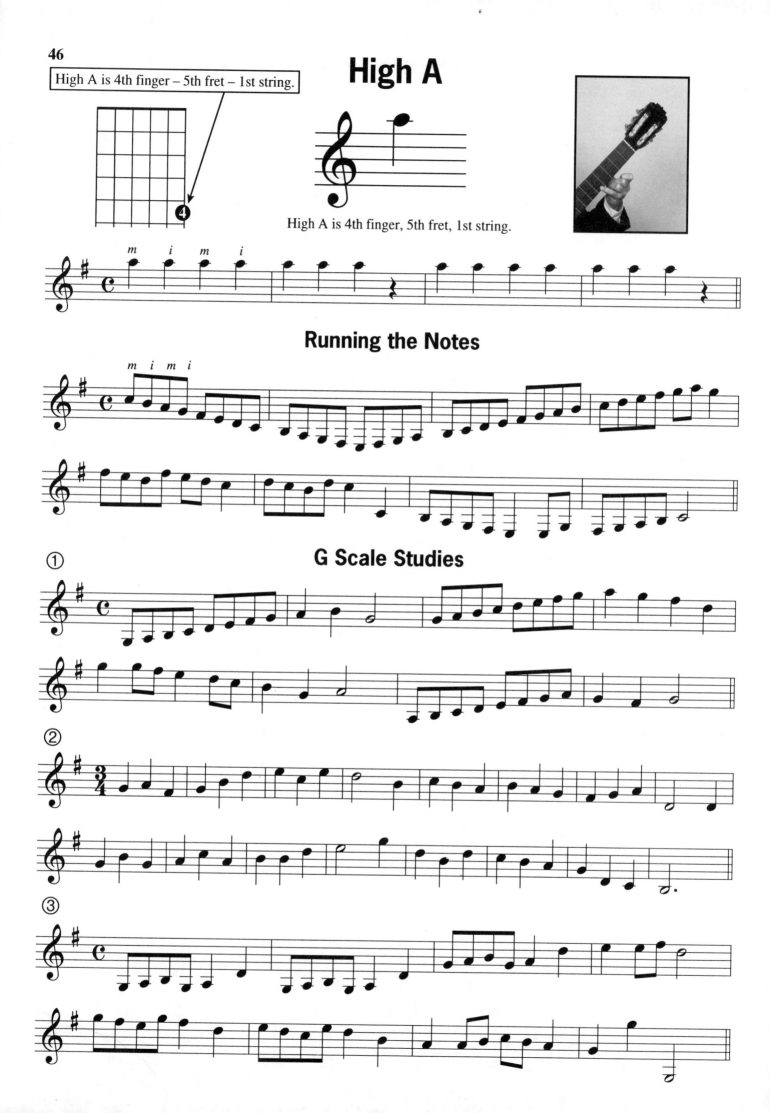

Auld Lang Syne

Finlandia Theme

Waltz by Chopin

German Hymn
(Duet)

Tr.93

means to hold the note